The Dominie Collection of Traditional Tales
For Young Readers

The Gingerbread Man

Retold by Alan Trussell-Cullen

Illustrated by Edward Mooney

Dominie Press, Inc.

There was once an old man and an old woman who loved to eat gingerbread. One day they made a Gingerbread Man. They rolled him out on the baking tray and put him in the oven to bake.

Soon the Gingerbread Man was baked. The old woman opened the oven door.

"Now we can eat our Gingerbread Man," said the old man.

But before they could do anything, the Gingerbread Man jumped out of the oven and said, "Run! Run! As fast as you can! You won't catch me! I'm the Gingerbread Man!"

4

The Gingerbread Man ran out of the house.
"Catch him!" cried the old man and the old woman,
and they ran after him.

5

The Gingerbread Man met up with a dog.

6

"Yum!" said the dog. "I think I'll eat this Gingerbread Man!" But the Gingerbread Man just laughed and said, "Run! Run! As fast as you can! You won't catch me! I'm the Gingerbread Man! I can run faster than an old woman and an old man, and I can run faster than you!"

So the dog joined in the chase.

Before long, the Gingerbread Man met a cow.

"Yum!" said the cow. "I think I'll eat this Gingerbread Man!"

But the Gingerbread Man just laughed and said, "Run! Run! As fast as you can! You won't catch me! I'm the Gingerbread Man! I can run faster than an old woman, faster than an old man, and faster than a dog. And I can run faster than you!"

So the cow joined in the chase, too.

The Gingerbread Man met a horse.

"Yum!" said the horse. "I think I'll eat this Gingerbread Man!"

But the Gingerbread Man just laughed and said, "Run! Run! As fast as you can! You won't catch me! I'm the Gingerbread Man! I can run faster than an old woman, faster than an old man, and faster than a dog or a cow. And I can run faster than you!"

So the horse joined in the chase, too.

The Gingerbread Man came to a river. Beside the river was a sly old fox.

"Gingerbread Man," said the fox. "Can I help you cross the river? Jump on my back and you won't get wet."
So the Gingerbread Man jumped on the fox's back.

When they were a quarter of the way across the
river, the sly old fox said, "Gingerbread Man, the river is
deeper here. Climb onto my head so you don't get wet."
So the Gingerbread Man climbed onto the fox's head.

When they were half-way across the river, the sly old fox said, "Gingerbread Man, the river is much deeper here. Climb onto my nose so you don't get wet."

So the Gingerbread Man climbed onto his nose.

13

When they were three-quarters of the way across the river, the sly old fox said, "Gingerbread Man, the river is very deep here. Climb into my mouth so you don't get wet."

So the Gingerbread Man climbed into the fox's mouth.

"Yum!" said the fox. "I love gingerbread!"
Snap went the fox's teeth!
And that was the end of the Gingerbread Man!